Carry Me Kat

A comedy

Rachel Musgrove

Samuel French — London
www.samuelfrench-london.co.uk

© 2010 BY RACHEL MUSGROVE

Rights of Performance by Amateurs are controlled by Samuel French Ltd, 52 Fitzroy Street, London W1T 5JR, and they, or their authorized agents, issue licences to amateurs on payment of a fee. **It is an infringement of the Copyright to give any performance or public reading of the play before the fee has been paid and the licence issued.**

The Royalty Fee indicated below is subject to contract and subject to variation at the sole discretion of Samuel French Ltd.

>   Basic fee for each and every
>   performance by amateurs   Code D
>   in the British Isles

The publication of this play does not imply that it is necessarily available for performance by amateurs or professionals, either in the British Isles or Overseas. Amateurs and professionals considering a production are strongly advised in their own interests to apply to the appropriate agents for written consent before starting rehearsals or booking a theatre or hall.

ISBN 978 0 573 12036 7

The right of Rachel Musgrove to be identified as author
of this work has been asserted by her in accordance with
Section 77 of the Copyright, Designs and Patents Act 1988.

Please see page iv for further copyright information

CARRY ME KATE

Carry Me Kate won Best Original Script at the Canberra Festival of One Act Plays in 2005. It was first performed at the Southern Cross Theatre with the following cast:

Kate	Rachel Musgrove
Dave	Cameron Baxter
Tash	Katherine Morgan
Mark	Andrew Musgrove
Waiter	
Kate's Father	Dave Jones
Priest	
Doctor	

Directed by Rachel Musgrove

COPYRIGHT INFORMATION
(See also page ii)

This play is fully protected under the Copyright Laws of the British Commonwealth of Nations, the United States of America and all countries of the Berne and Universal Copyright Conventions.

All rights, including Stage, Motion Picture, Radio, Television, Public Reading, and Translation into Foreign Languages, are strictly reserved.

No part of this publication may lawfully be reproduced in ANY form or by any means — photocopying, typescript, recording (including video-recording), manuscript, electronic, mechanical, or otherwise — or be transmitted or stored in a retrieval system, without prior permission.

Licences are issued subject to the understanding that it shall be made clear in all advertising matter that the audience will witness an amateur performance; that the names of the authors of the plays shall be included on all announcements and on all programmes; and that the integrity of the authors' work will be preserved.

The Royalty Fee is subject to contract and subject to variation at the sole discretion of Samuel French Ltd.

In Theatres or Halls seating Four Hundred or more the fee will be subject to negotiation.

In Territories Overseas the fee quoted in this Acting Edition may not apply. A fee will be quoted on application to our local authorized agent, or if there is no such agent, on application to Samuel French Ltd, London.

VIDEO-RECORDING OF AMATEUR PRODUCTIONS

Please note that the copyright laws governing video-recording are extremely complex and that it should not be assumed that any play may be video-recorded for *whatever purpose* without first obtaining the permission of the appropriate agents. The fact that a play is published by Samuel French Ltd does not indicate that video rights are available or that Samuel French Ltd controls such rights.

CHARACTERS

Kate, 20s
Dave, 20s, Kate's boyfriend
Tash, 20s, Kate's friend and Dave's neighbour
Mark, 20s, Dave's friend and flatmate
Waiter, French
Kate's Father (voice only)
Priest
Doctor

The Waiter, Priest, Kate's Father and the Doctor can all be played by the same actor

Time — the present

For Jill Bridgen

CARRY ME KATE

Scene 1

Four chairs line the stage. Kate and Dave sit on the middle two chairs and speak to the audience

Dave It was not my fault.
Kate I met him at a friend's party.
Dave Natasha, my neighbour, told me she was having a party.
Kate I didn't expect him to be there.
Dave I came around with the lads and a carton of beer.
Kate After all, it was a Tupperware party.
Dave We arrived to find plastic containers everywhere.
Kate I guess I was expecting … women.
Dave Then Natasha harped on about invites only.
Kate That's when I realized he was a snag.
Dave That's when I sat my backside down and stayed put. No woman tells me what to do!
Kate Sensitive new-age guy.
Dave Couldn't even watch the football. There were lunchboxes absolutely everywhere.
Kate Or maybe he was gay.
Dave So we did what we do best: drinking.
Kate He seemed to be flirting with his friends.
Dave Before long I was playing strip poker with the lads.
Kate Then I realized he was just confident.
Dave It was a funny night. Got right down to my underpants.
Kate Open-minded and confident.
Dave And then I noticed this woman.
Kate It was obvious he liked me.

Dave She looked all right from a distance.

Kate He kept on looking at me.

Dave (*squinting*) But you've got to check up close. You can never be too careful.

Kate And I swear I saw him wink.

Dave Especially after a few pints.

Kate And I thought it was cute.

Dave But I couldn't be bothered to get off the settee.

Kate So I winked back.

Dave And that was when she came over to me.

Kate And that was when he came over to me.

Dave I generally don't like women who make the first move.

Kate He said he wanted to get to know me.

Dave Wearing the trousers before they've even asked your name.

Kate To be honest, he seemed a bit desperate.

Dave But I gave her a chance.

Kate Tash had taught me that meant he was either rebounding, emotionally unstable or incapable of long-term relationships.

Dave I prepared myself for her to be a little ... simple.

Kate Then I thought, maybe he just liked me.

Dave To my surprise, I found her all right.

Kate We spoke for ages.

Dave Easy to have a conversation with.

Kate But he just kept on talking about himself and nothing else.

Dave We just spoke about normal things, work and interests.

Kate I started to wonder if he could only be handled in small doses.

Dave Normally women are just studying my face to figure out what our future children might look like.

Kate But as I said before, he seemed so confident.

Dave But she was different. Genuine.

Kate Fit.

Dave Funny.

Kate Outgoing.

Dave Intelligent.

Kate An all-round decent guy.

Dave I actually don't care about the intelligent thing but she was so ... anyway ...

Kate So when he asked me out.
Dave She got herself a date.
Kate I said yes.
Dave And I got a plastic container.
Kate I thought: what's the worst that can happen?
Dave Tight seal. Zipped-in freshness.
Kate But the first date was a little ... peculiar.

Scene 2

An expensive French restaurant. Kate and Dave are reading menus

Kate This restaurant is lovely.
Dave (*intimidated by the elaborate table setting*) Not shy of forks, are they?
Kate What will you order?
Dave I'm not sure. (*Reading the menu*) I wouldn't mind a pie and chips but I can't find it.
Kate (*laughing, then returning to her menu*) Such a wonderful cuisine.
Dave Fancy that — escargot! I've never actually seen that on a menu.
Kate I don't think you pronounce the T.
Dave Oh. You speak French?
Kate No.
Dave I speak a little myself. (*Beat*) *Voulez-vous coucher avec moi ce soir?*
Kate No.

There is an awkward moment. They both stare at their menus

I think I'll have the marinated octopus for starters. The chicken looks nice for main. Or the wild roast stuffed goose with organic prunes in Armagnac with golden crisp sage potato boulangères and seasonal homegrown steamed vegetables.

Dave reads the menu ... then notices the prices! He subtly checks how much money he has in his wallet

A French Waiter enters

Waiter (*to Kate*) Mademoiselle, it is not so often we are so lucky to have such a beautiful woman here. I think you are why the stars have come out tonight. No?

Kate (*embarrassed*) Surely not.

Waiter Ah, but surely so. For many evenings now I have just barely made out the moon, yet tonight the entire universe has aligned such a spectacular show for us. For you. And me.

Dave (*after a pause*) And Dave.

Waiter (*still looking at Kate*) And what?

Dave And Dave.

Waiter (*to Kate*) Ah, yes, David, he is your husband? Boyfriend? ... Lover?

Kate Well, it's ... he's ...

Dave On Facebook we're "it's complicated".

Waiter Ah, yes, the British man — he complicates.

Dave Shall we order?

Waiter The French man, he romanticizes. I am not sure if this is even a word in English.

Dave I think I'm ready to order. Kate?

Kate Ah, yes. Um, I'd like the marinated octopus please, and a small serving of the goose for main.

Waiter Such an intelligent choice.

Dave (*conscious of the price*) I'd better just have the soup I think.

Waiter (*apathetically*) The aubergine soup is probably OK. For you. Warm, I guess.

There is an uncomfortable silence

And the main course?

Dave Um, OK. Steak. But instead of the (*reading the menu*) ... caramelized onion and sautéed champignons ... can I just get chips?

Scene 2

Waiter (*pretending to laugh*) Ah, the British humour. (*Deadly serious*) It kills me.

The Waiter exits

Kate and Dave both look around the restaurant

Dave The French can be so ... French.

There is another awkward silence

So, how do you know Natasha?
Kate We do yoga together.
Dave Yoga? That's like karma sutra, isn't it? But you wear leggings.
Kate (*not wanting to be rude*) Yes ... leggings ... that's the main difference.
Dave Mmn. Interesting.
Kate You should come some time.
Dave Yes ... I think I'm busy that night.
Kate Which night?
Dave Which night did you say it was?
Kate I hadn't yet.
Dave Oh, no, yes, it's just that I am busy most nights.
Kate It's fine if you don't want to go.
Dave No, I do. I'd love to ... I love yoga ... it's just that I'm ... studying.
Kate Oh. What are you studying?
Dave (*lying*) Ah—t. Art.
Kate An artist, hey?
Dave Well, I dabble.
Kate Impressive. Who's your favourite?
Dave What?
Kate Artist. Who's your favourite artist?
Dave Umm, no favourites, really. They're all good.

The Waiter enters, stands at the ready near their table and looks suggestively at Kate

Kate Perhaps I'll have another drink.

Dave slides the bottle towards Kate. The Waiter comes over and fills her glass, but not Dave's. He returns to his position, not taking his eyes off Kate

Dave (*for want of something to say*) Yes, eat, drink and be merry, for tomorrow you shall die.

Kate What's that supposed to mean?

Dave Nothing, really, I don't actually think you're going to die tomorrow ... and if you do don't blame me. But chances are you won't, if it makes you feel any better.

Kate (*sarcastically*) Yes, feels lovely.

Dave That came out wrong. (*Topping up Kate's glass of wine*) What I meant to say is get yourself as drunk as you like. Fine by me. I won't tell anybody. I never kiss and tell.

Kate We've never kissed.

Dave No, I'm talking about all the other girls ... I met them all before I met you ... That also came out wrong.

Kate I wonder how much longer dinner will be.

Dave (*taking the wine bottle and pouring himself a glass*) I might have a drink myself.

Kate So, you've dated a lot of women?

Dave No, no, no it's not like that at all. I've hardly dated anyone. I mean, there have been a few, just a good, round number, that's all. I didn't mean what I said before. Sorry, I'm a little nervous.

Kate Don't be. We're just two friends sharing a meal. That's all.

Dave Oh. So we're just friends?

Kate I don't know.

Dave Well, this is awkward, isn't it?

Kate (*after a pause*) Yeah.

Dave I'd consider myself quite lucky if you were to be my girlfriend.

Kate (*smiling*) Would you now?

Dave Yeah, I really would.

Kate (*raising her glass*) Well, I guess that's it then. We are officially on a date.

The Waiter sighs and is no longer interested in Kate

Dave (*relieved*) Oh, good, because I've already told the lads you're my girlfriend. (*He clinks his glass against Kate's*)
Kate What?
Dave What?
Kate Talk about kiss and tell.
Dave Sorry. I was just excited.
Kate So what did your friends think?
Dave About what?
Kate About us? About me?
Dave Um, I don't think they thought at all really.
Kate What have you told them about me?
Dave Um. Good things, mainly.
Kate Like what?
Dave Um, well. To tell the truth, I don't really know you that well … Which is why I'm excited about getting to know you.
Kate All right, let's get to know each other. Do you prefer night or day?
Dave Day.
Kate Blue or red?
Dave Blue.
Kate Cats or dogs?
Dave Dogs.
Kate Summer or winter?
Dave Summer.
Kate (*laughing*) I feel like I know you already.

Scene 3

The gym

Tash and Kate are continuing their love-hate relationships with the Stairmaster

Tash Tell me, tell me, tell me, tell me, tell me!
Kate There's nothing to tell.
Tash There's always something to tell.
Kate He's just a nice fellow.
Tash Just a nice fellow, is he? That doesn't sound like the full report to me.
Kate There's nothing to report.
Tash (*after a pause*) Now I *know* there's something. So, are you going to see him again?
Kate Maybe.
Tash Maybe, what does that mean?
Kate (*after a pause*) Day, blue, dogs, summer ... Virgo.
Tash Virgo?
Kate Virgo.

Devastated, Tash presses the emergency stop button on her Stairmaster and sinks to the floor

Tash I'm so sorry. But it's not an entirely lost cause we have here, just needs a little more work than first anticipated, that's all. The main thing is you don't want to analyze him. It's too early. So, get me a pen, let's make a list.

Scene 4

Mark and Dave's flat. Mark and Dave are watching TV

Mark Rubbish!
Dave Are those players asleep or what?
Mark They're always bloomin' sleeping!
Dave Yeah, well, you're the one who keeps backing them, Mark.
Mark Tell me about it. They're costing me a small fortune. But they'll turn good. They'll win me a packet one of these days. I guarantee you.
Dave How do you know?
Mark Probability, Dave, probability.

Scene 4

Dave Is that why you do the Lotto as well?

Mark (*laughing*) Listen here, when I'm stinking rich I'll remember to forget you first.

Dave Won't be easy. I'll be a famous golfer by then. (*Pause*) You know, in ten years' time we'll probably still be here.

Mark Great.

Dave Doing this.

Mark Brilliant!

Dave Don't you ever think about the future?

Mark (*very cautious*) What are you talking about?

Dave The future.

Mark What has got you bringing the F-word into my house? It's that Katherine, isn't it?

Dave Kate did mention it.

Mark I bet she did.

Dave Don't worry. I wasn't listening to her.

Mark Good, Dave, good. Don't listen. That's the best thing you can do. If you listen you're only going to hear the wrong things.

Dave Probably.

Mark And why on earth is she saying the F-word after five weeks anyway?

Dave It's been six months.

Mark Five weeks, six months … It's hardly future stuff, is it?

Dave I guess not. It's just that I really like her, and ——

Mark I'm not listening to this, Oprah.

Dave C'mon, Mark, I just need to talk about it.

Mark Talk? Future?

Dave I didn't say both of those, did I?

Mark I'm afraid so. I felt like I was making a commitment just listening to you.

Dave What do I do?

Mark There's plenty of fish in the sea. That's what you must keep reminding them.

Scene 5

Kate and Tash are in a yoga class

Tash He didn't say that!
Kate He did.
Tash You are just a big fish in a small pond with that man.
Kate Perhaps, but I don't think he meant it. I think he is afraid.
Tash Afraid of what?
Kate Well, I've organized a mini-break.
Tash (*excited*) A mini-break! You realize this is an absolutely huge deal, don't you?
Kate It's just a weekend away.
Tash Oh, no, it's bigger. It's big. It's a test, a rehearsal … a dress rehearsal.
Kate It's more of a getaway, really.
Tash Hun, your ears are there but they're not working. There is really nothing mini about the mini-break. It's the ultimate test to see whether or not he is your life partner … whether or not your souls will intertwine, joining your most hidden thoughts and deepest secrets. It's the be-all and end-all of whether or not you're ever going to make it in the long run. The pressure's on. (*Pause*) So, where are you going?

Scene 6

Dave and Kate address the audience

Dave So I laid my foot down.
Kate I booked a trip to the Lake District.
Dave I said, look, Kate, no more talking about the future.
Kate Stayed in a gorgeous stone cottage.
Dave And no more talking about talking.
Kate With a view over Lake Windermere.
Dave In fact, don't even mention the word "talk".
Kate It was so beautiful and romantic.

Dave Let's just take things slowly.
Kate Bottle of wine.
Dave So we agreed to take things nice and slow again.
Kate Little love heart chocolates.
Dave We were back to just slowly heading nowhere.
Kate We were really heading somewhere now.
Dave I was back in the driver's seat.
Kate Just the two of us.
Dave And it was my decision to drive us up to the Lake District.
Kate And a tremendous selection of wine and cheese.

Scene 7

Kate is driving Dave's car, creeping along at a snail's pace

Sound effects to indicate that it's raining cats and dogs outside and leaking on to Dave's head inside

Dave Maybe I should drive.
Kate I'm not putting up with any more of your Chinese water torture.
Dave (*obviously very annoyed by the leak*) It's not that bad.
Kate Anyway, I'm happy to drive. You go too fast.
Dave It's funny you mention the speed. I was just going to bring that up myself. You can always accelerate a little more if you'd like. We seem to be creeping along rather slowly.
Kate It's raining.
Dave Yes, you've got the windscreen wipers on full pelt. Any faster and they'll fly right off.
Kate I'd barely be able to see a thing.
Dave I've twenty-twenty vision.
Kate I thought you had reading glasses.
Dave They're for reading, not for driving.
Kate You've got to read to drive. You've got to read the speed signs.
Dave I can. They read fifty miles per hour.
Kate Yes, dear.

Dave You're doing thirty-four.
Kate Yes, dear.

Dave fiddles about with the radio

Dave No reception. Brilliant.
Kate Not to worry, we'll be there soon.
Dave At this rate by the time we get there it'll be time to leave.
Kate Don't be silly. It'll be lovely. This rain can't last forever, and we've got all that lovely wine and cheese.
Dave Wine?
Kate It's in the back.

Dave scrambles around the back seat trying to get a bottle of wine

Dave Any beer?
Kate You can't have beer and cheese.
Dave I could try.
Kate Well, I only packed wine. We can stop somewhere for some beer.
Dave Don't stop. We've just started rolling forward. Barely.
Kate Tell you what, pass the CD on the seat there, please.

Dave passes Kate the CD and brings a bottle of wine and a plastic wine glass to his lap. Kate puts the CD in the CD player

An irritatingly catchy popular song plays

Dave tosses the glass on to the back seat and swigs out of the bottle

Dave (*sarcastically*) Perfect!

The music stops. Rain and dripping sound effects cut out

Scene 8

Kate and Dave address the audience

Kate It was perfect!
Dave I thought I'd died and gone to hell.
Kate The weekend just flew by.
Dave So I drank myself stupid.
Kate We both had the best time.
Dave I don't normally drink wine.
Kate We really got to bond on a deeper level.
Dave So I got a little more sloshed than I intended to.
Kate And understand one another's soul.
Dave Couldn't see straight and all the rest of it.
Kate It really strengthened our relationship.
Dave And walking … I wasn't even going to attempt it!
Kate I was surprised at how quickly things were moving.
Dave My feet just weren't working.
Kate But it still felt right.
Dave I toppled right over.
Kate Which is why I wasn't all that surprised …
Dave I was on the ground, trying to get myself back up.
Kate When he got down on one knee …
Dave And I said to Kate …
Kate And proposed!
Dave I said, "Kate, will you carry me?"
Kate And of course I said yes. Yes, yes, yes!
Dave She said she would, then got all excited and started jumping up and down. I guess she was a little drunk herself because she never bothered to help me up in the end.

Scene 9

Mark and Dave's apartment

Mark (*bitterly*) You missed a call while you were out.

Dave Did I?
Mark (*very slowly*) Tash. Rang.
Dave Tash?
Mark She's a friend of Kate's.
Dave Kate's friend? What was she after?
Mark She wanted to say congratulations.
Dave (*only half listening*) Oh, all right.
Mark She heard about Kate's engagement.
Dave (*confused*) Kate's engagement?
Mark To you.
Dave (*shocked*) To me?
Mark When were you planning on telling me all of this?
Dave Probably once I knew about all of this!
Mark Tash said, (*imitating Tash*) "Ooh, I'm so excited about the flower decorations for Kate and Dave's wedding. Pass on my congratulations to the groom. Isn't it just the best news ever?"
Dave And she definitely said Dave?
Mark No doubt about it.
Dave No surname?

Scene 10

Kate's house. Kate and Tash

Tash Ooh, I'm so excited about the flower decorations for your wedding. Congratulations. Isn't it just the best news ever!
Kate I can't wait to go wedding dress shopping.
Tash Fur.
Kate Fur?
Tash Off the shoulder faux fur. It's in.
Kate Um. OK. Where can I get some? And what shall I do with my hair?
Tash Don't worry, we'll have a hair rehearsal.
Kate Of course we'll have a hair rehearsal, but how should we be rehearsing it?

Tash As it just so happens, (*fetching a gigantic folder*) this is all merely a rough draft but I think there are some good concepts. It is alphabetized but essentially we've got: reception venues, flower arrangements, invitation designs, dress details, car hire, DJs... There's so much to organize. And it could all be very easily undone by one single mistake in the seating plan.

Kate The seating plan?

Tash Nobody wants to get stuck next to fat Uncle Fred while he's talking about his sticky divorce proceedings all night. You've got to set it out in a friendly way. We've got shoes — that's a big one! — hymns, vows ... I've always thought it really beautiful to write your own vows. It's so personal and touching, the greatest gift you can give, the most beautiful promise you can make. It's like laying an invisible path from your heart to his, untouchable, for all eternity ... (*handing Kate a sheet of paper*) so I've written your personal vows for you. Then there's jewellery, make-up, ushers, I mean, this is your day to shine, Kate. This is your big day! (*Pause*) And this is how I see it happening.

Kate But what about Dave?

Tash Dave? Oh, don't worry, we'll get him to come over and help us with these mags. (*She hands Kate a pile of bridal magazines*)

Scene 11

Mark and Dave's apartment

Dave I thought they meant mags for her car.

Mark Of course.

Dave But they meant magazines full of fit ladies dressed like ridiculous, white marshmallows. I wasted my entire Friday night looking at models, who I had to pretend were too skinny, and help choose which hair style went with which dress.

Mark There's only so much you can do with hair.

Dave I know. You brush it, you wash it. Although for the wedding I'm thinking of using that conditioner stuff.

Mark What? So you *are* getting married? I thought you were going around there to ask her where on earth she got the idea from that you two were getting married.
Dave I was.
Mark And ...

SCENE 12

Kate's house. Kate and Dave

Dave Kate.
Kate (*lovestruck*) Davey Baby.
Dave Remember when you announced our engagement?
Kate Like it was yesterday.
Dave It was yesterday.
Kate Oh yeah ... Fuzzy Wuzzy.
Dave Fuzzy Wuzzy?
Kate Fuzzy Wuzzy Pookie Bear.
Dave Umm, OK. Anyway, Kate, look, there's something I need to talk to you about.
Kate Me too!
Dave No, this is really urgent.
Kate (*dialling a number on her mobile phone*) So's mine. Daddy really wants to talk to you.
Dave Your father?
Kate Yeah. He said it was a matter of life and death.
Dave But, Kate, can I just first ——
Kate It's ringing. Here you go, Baby Cakes. (*She hands him the phone*) How exciting. It's my daddy. It's your daddy ... It's our daddy!
Dave (*into the phone*) ... Umm, hello?
Dad (*from the phone*) Listen here, son, I don't know who you are or why the heck you didn't ask my permission about all this ——
Dave Because Kate didn't ask mine!
Dad But the one thing it does tell me is that you've got bollocks.
Dave (*petrified*) Yes, sir. Two of them.
Dad And I hope they aren't what's caused all this!

Dave What? No, they've kept out of ... trouble.
Dad So she isn't pregnant?
Dave No, sir.
Dad And this isn't a shotgun wedding?
Dave No, sir.
Dad Good, because if I find out it is, I won't be afraid to pull the trigger. Nobody — but nobody — lets my little girl down. Understood?
Dave Yes, sir.

Kate's father hangs up

Kate What did Daddy want?
Dave Oh, he ... just wanted ... to say congratulations.
Kate Of course he did! Everyone is saying it. This is so wonderful. You've made me so happy, Dave. This is going to be the best day of our lives!
Dave (*unconvinced*) Yeah. Of course.

Scene 13

Dave and Mark are at a golf driving range

Dave You don't understand. The man is Hitler.
Mark So what?
Dave So I don't want to mess with Hitler.
Mark I'd rather take on Hitler than a wife. Marriages take more lives than wars. Can't you see what's happening here? She's taking over. They all are. Women are taking over the world ... one man at a time. Well, they are not going to take me ... (*Looking to the sky*) They're not going to take me.
Dave It's not all that bad. After all, I do love her. I don't mind being with her ... it's just that forever sounds like an awfully long time.
Mark This really is a pickle you've got yourself in. An over-sized, hormone-pumped pickle. I don't want to see you changing. I don't want to see you having dinner parties. You must stay focused,

stay strong. You must take it one day at a time. Starting with the wedding day.

Scene 14

The church. Wedding music plays

Tash walks down the aisle, followed by Kate, towards the Priest. Tash is wearing a hideous shawl and Kate is wearing an elaborate faux fur poncho. They are holding bouquets and smiling ecstatically ... until they realize Dave is not there. They are not impressed

Meanwhile

Dave (*to the audience*) I mean, seriously, the woman looked at so many bloomin' churches before she made up her mind. How was I supposed to remember which one she'd finally chosen? I had to ring her father's mobile. He wasn't too impressed. Everyone said I should have read the invitation, but Kate never thought to send me one. And just quietly, no one ever said anything about how rude it was of her father to have his phone on in the church.

Dave and Mark arrive at the church unfashionably late. They walk down the aisle together, very self-conscious, speaking through false grins

Mark Why does my tie look like a strip of carpet?
Dave Because it has to match the bridesmaid's dress.
Mark Shouldn't you walk down the aisle with Kate?
Dave Yes.
Mark (*amused*) You are in trouble. (*Noticing Kate*) What on earth is that?
Dave I think it's Kate.
Mark What's she wearing?
Dave It may or may not be a piece of roadkill.

Mark For crying out loud. Carpets and roadkill.

Dave and Mark reach the altar. Mark reluctantly hands Dave over to Kate. It's hard to tell if she wants him

Dave Better late than never.
Kate Never again.
Dave Don't worry. I'll be on time for my next wedding. (*Trying to laugh it off*) Not now?
Kate Not ever, Dave.
Priest Are we quite ready? (*Clearing his throat*)

The music fades

Dearly Beloved, we are gathered here today to celebrate the wedding of Katherine and David, as they begin their journey of lifelong commitment, for the rest of their lives, forever, until death do them part. Forever. Every morning from today onwards you will be waking up to this woman's face as she wears less and less make-up for you and grows older and wider, proving every law of gravity. So long as you both shall live. Forever. Forever. Forever.
Kate I do.
Priest And David. Do you take this woman to be your lawfully wedded wife?
Dave Sure. Why not?
Priest And now by the powers invested in me by the Stonehenge National Democratic Pagan Committee, I pronounce you husband and wife. You may kiss the bride.

Dave leans in to kiss Kate. Kate only offers him her cheek. Tash leads Kate to their chairs

Lively music and background chatter can be heard. They are now at the wedding reception

A tipsy Mark taps his glass with a fork, hinting for Dave to give a speech. Dave doesn't want to. Mark keeps tinking

The music and background chatter fades. Beaten, Dave stands to propose a toast

Mark tinks one final, inappropriate time

Dave Um, hello everyone. Family, friends, people I don't even know … Thanks for coming to our wedding. It really means a lot to us. Sorry I was late … Umm … I guess I'd like to thank Kate for waiting … and for being a wonderful wife. Actually it's only been a few hours and already I can feel that I'll be sleeping on the settee tonight. Better get used to that. I should have put a sofa-bed on the wedding list. (*He laughs nervously*) But it's worth it. After all, I do love you Kate, and I always will … most probably. Well, actually, the odds are against us. There's a seventy per cent divorce rate these days. But I'm pretty sure that won't be us. In fact I think that's only in America and ours is sixty-forty. So, here's to us being in the minority. (*Raising his glass*) To the minority! (*He drinks until the glass is completely empty*)

Mark (*enthusiastically raising his glass*) To the minority!

Scene 15

Kate and Dave address the audience

Kate I could write a book about all the idiotic things he's said.
Dave I was worried my wedding speech was a little unpolished.
Kate And still never finish it.
Dave But Kate didn't mind at all.
Kate I could fill an entire library.
Dave She was smitten.
Kate But when you're in love, no matter how cross you are …
Dave Absolutely smitten.
Kate You can never stay cross for long.
Dave She was more in love with me than ever.
Kate And soon we were back on track.
Dave Because I was taking her …

Kate And on the plane.
Dave To Barcelona!
Kate To Barcelona!

Scene 16

Cheesy inflight music plays in the background

Kate and Dave sit side by side on the plane

Kate The seats are a little squishy.
Dave What do you expect for eighteen pounds return?
Kate Not much, just to be able to sit.
Dave We'll be there in no time.
Kate We've been two hours on the runway.
Dave They are just clearing to leave.
Kate That's exactly what they said two hours ago.
Dave Just think, all the money we saved on flights can go towards more sangria!
Kate Now you're talking!
Dave Barcelona!
Kate Barcelona!
Dave Beaches.
Kate Architecture.
Dave Cocktails.
Kate Salsa dancing.
Dave Sex.
Kate (*after a pause*) We'll see.
Dave (*in a deep voice*) Good evening ladies and gentlemen. This is your Captain Dave speaking. In just under two hours we'll be landing on the beautiful shores of España. I ask that you each put your tables in their upright position, fasten your seatbelts, and please, enjoy your stay.
Kate Roger that. Over and out.

The music stops

Kate moves to one side. Kate and Dave speak to the audience

Dave I had a tremendous time on the honeymoon.
Kate It was the worst week of my life.
Dave Absolutely tremendous!
Kate I still had some imported Bangladeshi flowers in my hair that Tash insisted on having at the wedding.
Dave Bit of a shame about Kate though.
Kate And the customs officials seemed to think they would damage the Spanish ecosystem.
Dave She really missed out.
Kate I said, fine, fine, take the flowers.
Dave Really, really missed out.
Kate But that wasn't enough for them.
Dave Swimming.
Kate They wanted to quarantine my whole head!
Dave Snorkelling.
Kate I was only supposed to be there for an hour or two.
Dave Cable car rides.
Kate But they sat me next to this diseased little infant.
Dave Gaudi tours.
Kate And I broke out in a rash.
Dave Belly dancing.
Kate By the time I was allowed out we were due to head home.
Dave Hula hooping.
Kate And I hadn't even left the airport!
Dave Kite flying.
Kate Dave said he'd make it up to me with some duty free shopping.
Dave Bikini contest judging.
Kate But when we got to the shops our credit card was maxed out.
Dave Snake charming.
Kate He said he didn't know where all the money went.
Dave Drinking.
Kate But I knew.